# Victorian Britain
# Resource Book

## Contents

# Queen Victoria

On 20 June 1837, at 6 o'clock in the morning,
two important men arrived at Kensington Palace in London.
They had come to tell Princess Victoria, who was
only eighteen years old, that her uncle, King William, had
died in the night and that she was now a queen.

An artist painted this picture of the
moment when Victoria was given the news.

The visitors have kneeled down to
kiss the Queen's hand. They did this to show her
that she was now the true and lawful ruler.

Three years after she became Queen, Victoria married a German Prince called Albert. Victoria kept a diary and often wrote in it about her happy family life. Like most people who lived then, Victoria and Albert had a large family. They had nine children altogether. You can see them with the first five in this painting.

**Find:**

- **Queen Victoria and Prince Albert. How did the artist show that they were very fond of each other?**

- **their eldest child, Princess Vicky. She is on the right-hand side of the picture.**

- **their sons, Prince Albert Edward and Prince Alfred. They are on the left-hand side of the picture. In Victorian times some little boys wore dresses. Albert Edward, who was also called the Prince of Wales, is next to his mother to show that he will be the next king.**

- **Princess Alice and the new baby, Princess Helena.**

Prince Albert died in 1861 so, for most of her reign, Victoria was a **widow**. After his death she usually chose black clothes to wear.

**Widow**

A woman whose husband has died.

This portrait was painted in 1900, a year before Victoria died, when she was an old lady of 81.

Queen Victoria was not only Queen of England and Wales, Scotland and Ireland. She ruled over 'Britain beyond the seas' — the countries in the British **Empire**. These included Canada, Australia, New Zealand, Jamaica, India and many countries in Africa. In 1876 she was made Empress of India.

In 1887, when she had been on the throne for fifty years, people all round the Empire celebrated her Golden **Jubilee**.

**Can you see the Queen on her Golden Jubilee in an open carriage drawn by horses?**

Many of her children had married princes and princesses from European Royal families by this time. They are all in this special Golden Jubilee painting.

**Find:**

- her eldest son, the Prince of Wales. He is in the middle of the picture.

- two of her daughters, Princess Victoria and Princess Helena. They were both mothers themselves and are sitting near the Queen.

- the Queen's grandchildren. How many can you see?

**Empire**

A group of countries ruled by one of them.

**Jubilee**

A special anniversary, such as a 25th or 50th one.

During Victoria's reign there were many new inventions. One of them was the camera, but there were no films to take colour photographs.

Here are some photos from the Queen's family album. There are four generations of the family in each picture.

**Queen Victoria with her daughter Beatrice, her grand-daughter Victoria and her great-grand-daughter Alice. When she grew up Alice had a son called Philip who is the Duke of Edinburgh, husband of Queen Elizabeth II, today.**

**Queen Victoria with her eldest son's family.**

**Find :**

- **her eldest son. He became King Edward VII when she died.**

- **her grandson. He became King George V.**

- **her great-grandson, the baby in the photo. He became King George VI and was the father of Queen Elizabeth II.**

# Towns and Cities

### Iron and Steam

At the beginning of Queen Victoria's reign most people in Britain lived and worked in the country, but by 1900 most lived and worked in a town or city. By then, many things which had once been made in people's homes were **mass-produced** by machines in mills and factories.

This painting shows men at work in Newcastle.
They are making a railway engine.

**Find:**

- the heavy hammers that the men used to beat the hot iron into shape.

- the picture of the engine they were making.

- an iron crane for lifting the pieces of iron.

- a little girl with her dad's lunch in a bowl.

- a train going over a new iron bridge. Trains still use it today.

---

### Mass-produced

**Using machines to make many things, all looking the same, instead of making one thing, by hand, at home.**

Towns like Sheffield expanded in the nineteenth century because of the discovery that steam could drive engines. Some engines drove machines; some engines on wheels pulled trains.

The engines were made of iron, which came from a rock called ironstone melted by fire in huge furnaces.

**This picture shows men collecting the melted iron from furnaces in Cwmbran in Wales. Boys and girls aged between 7 and 10 were paid to open and shut the furnace doors.**

**Furnace**

**A container made of iron which could hold a lot of heat.**

## Factories and Coal Mines

Some of the first machines were used to make cloth in cotton mills in Lancashire. Spinning machines spun the cotton into thread. After spinning, cloth was woven from the thread on a machine called a 'loom'.

The picture makes the factory look a pleasant place, but how true a picture was it? The machines were noisy, smelly and dangerous and were never stopped.

**Find:**

- **the pulley wheels. They were connected to the engine room. The engine drove all the pulleys.**

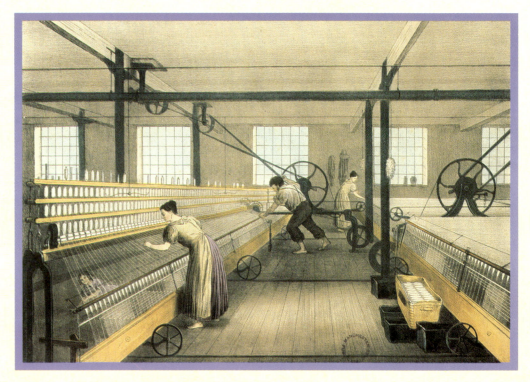

**These mill workers, painted in 1874, were allowed out for lunch. The women are eating their lunch in the street as there were no canteens in Victorian factories.**

The factories and mills needed a good supply of coal to keep the machines going. Gangs of coal miners, some of them women and children, worked underground. They were paid for the amount of coal they could get up to the surface, not for the number of hours they worked.

Working in the mines was dangerous. The underground passages were very low and narrow. A lot of the time the miners worked in the dark. Sometimes the mines flooded with water or part of the roof fell in.

These pictures were drawn by government inspectors from descriptions given by people who worked underground.

Find:

- miners pushing and pulling coal in trolleys along dark underground passages.

- a boy called a 'trapper boy' opening and shutting the trap door from one part of the mine to another. This was to stop dangerous gases spreading through the mine.

- candles used to help light up the mine. Sometimes these made the gases explode.

Stories about the bad working conditions in mines and factories soon got out to important people in government. They did not like what they heard at all. The factory and mine owners had been able to treat the workers as they liked. Parliament passed new laws to try and improve the lives of the workers.

The new laws said that:

- No child under the age of eight is to work in a factory or mine.

- Women are not to work underground.

- Children between the ages of eight and thirteen must only work for six and a half hours a day.

- Women and older children are not to work longer than ten hours a day.

- Factory inspectors will regularly visit factories to inspect working conditions.

Some women who lived near coal mines did not want to give up their jobs. They became known as 'pit brow lassies' as they now worked at the top of the pit. They had to put the coal through a wire sieve to separate the big lumps from the small.

The pit brow lassies also wore tough wooden shoes called 'clogs', and hats to keep the coal dust out of their hair.

# Trade Unions

By the middle of Queen Victoria's reign almost everything people needed could be made in a factory. To help each other, most workers in the same trade or job decided to combine together in clubs called Trade Unions. This way they were strong enough to demand better working conditions and safety in the workplace.

This is a membership certificate for the engineering workers who joined a Trade Union.

**Find:**

- the name of the Trade Union.

- the space for the member's name to be written.

- the six small pictures of things made by the workers in this Union.

- the Union motto. Why was it important for them to 'be united'?

- portraits of some of the first engineers. One of them is James Watt who discovered that steam power could drive engines; another is Richard Arkwright who invented a spinning machine.

- factory chimneys, a railway train and a steam ship.

# Workers' Homes

When the first factories were opened, millions of families had to move to where they could find work. Houses were quickly put up near the factories in 'terraces' with no space between one house and the next. Some of the terraces were also joined to the row behind and were called 'back to back' houses.

Most workers' houses had only four rooms and a cellar. The outside toilet, was with other families. There were no gardens only yards. This drawing shows some houses in London.

**In this picture you can see some workers' houses built in Leeds.**

**Find:**

- **the houses where the workers lived.**

- **the factories with their smoking chimneys.**

**Find:**

- **the back yards in this picture.**

- **a train puffing dirty smoke.**

- **the people in some of the back yards. Families were larger in Victorian times than they are today and these houses were very overcrowded.**

- **barrels for collecting rainwater.**

The bad housing and overcrowding meant that people could not keep themselves clean. Many did not even have a cold water tap in their house. Diseases like cholera and typhoid fever spread very quickly.

**This drawing shows what it was like inside a poor family's home. Most of the family has fallen ill. There is only one bed for nine people. Some have to sleep on the floor.**

The government decided to introduce some laws about public health. Town Councils had to put in proper drains and water pipes and to provide clean drinking water.

Big pumping stations for getting rid of waste and sewage were built, as well as public bath houses and wash houses. Those people who had no bathroom in their house could get a hot bath at the bath house and do their washing in the public wash house.

## Public Buildings

Many towns and cities became well-known for the things made there.

- Manchester became the centre of the cotton industry.

- Woollen cloth was made in Leeds and Bradford.

- Machine factories and heavy engineering works were built in Birmingham.

- Sheffield made the best cutlery in the world.

- Part of Staffordshire became known as the 'Potteries' because of the cups, saucers, plates, tiles and drainage pipes that were made there.

- Sunderland became a centre for glassmaking.

- In Swindon they made locomotives.

Some factory owners, as well as Town Councils cared about the environment. Sir Titus Salt, from Bradford, was one who built a model town for his workers. He used his own name and the name of the local river, the Aire, for the name of the town, Saltaire.

**This picture shows a big park, built in Saltaire, where families went walking on Sunday afternoons.**

Fine public buildings were built in all the big cities. This painting shows St George's Hall in Liverpool which was finished in 1854. Like the Greeks, the Victorians were proud of their cities and often copied their designs. Inside St George's Hall was a concert hall and a law court.

**Find :**

• **the decorated stone columns all round the hall, which is designed like a Greek temple.**

• **a bus drawn by horses.**

Many other public buildings for the whole community were built in Victorian times and are still used today. These included :

• Town halls, like the one in this picture.

• Hospitals.

• Workhouses for the unemployed.

• New factories.

• Schools and universities.

• Law courts and prisons.

• Railway stations.

• Banks and offices.

• Docks and harbours.

• Cemeteries outside the town where the dead were buried.

# The British Empire

Every 24th of May,
Victorian children at school
celebrated Empire Day.
The British Empire was the
largest the world has ever known,
even bigger than the
Roman Empire.

This is Maharajah Dalip Singh, an Indian prince whose father had been persuaded to co-operate with the British.

Find:

- the turban on his head. Dalip Singh was a Sikh.

- the painting of Queen Victoria which he wore on his pearl necklace. Queen Victoria paid for the painting. The British Raj ran India until 1947, when it became independent.

### Raj

**This came from a Hindi word meaning king.**

There were countries in the British Empire in every continent The Victorians were proud of saying that 'the sun never set on the Empire', which meant that it was always daytime in one country or another. Children learnt geography from a map hung on the wall which showed all the countries of the Empire coloured in red.

This plate was on sale as a souvenir for Queen Victoria's Golden Jubilee in 1887.

**Find:**

- Queen Victoria and her eldest son the Prince of Wales.

- the map of the world with some countries in the Empire coloured red. How many names of the countries do you know?

- the clock with the words 'the Empire on which the sun never sets'.

The names of some of the towns and cities in the Empire are round the clock. Find them on a map of the world:

| | | | |
|---|---|---|---|
| Cape Town | Natal | Aden | Victoria |
| Bombay | Calcutta | Ottawa | Hong Kong |
| Adelaide | Sydney | Aukland | Fiji |

## Empire Trade

Britain, Italy, France, Germany, Spain and Portugal all had Empires in the nineteenth century. Why did they control lands in other continents? One reason was to do with buying and selling.

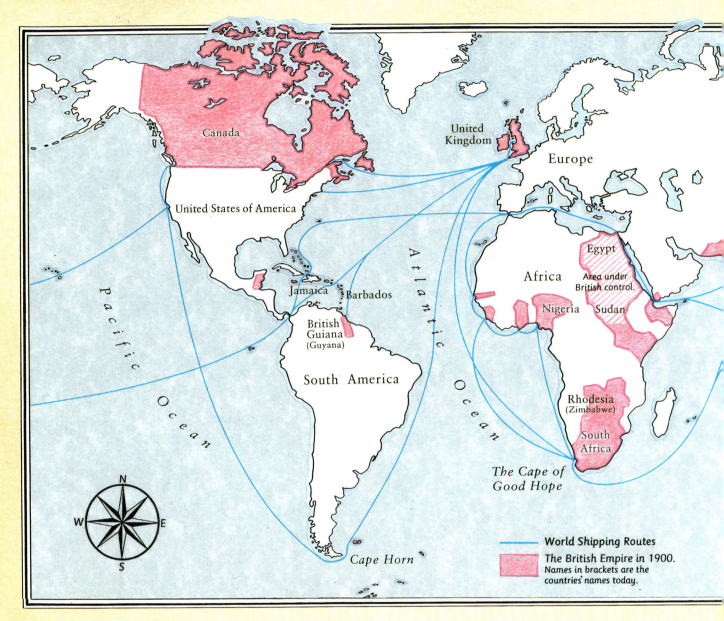

This map shows the routes taken by ships round the world. **Raw materials** from countries in the Empire were important to Britain. The British got them at a cheap price. Some of the raw materials like tea and coffee were sold over the counter in shops; some were sent to factories where they were made into cloth, soap, carpets and metal goods. Some of these factory **products**, such as cotton cloth, were then sold back to the countries which the raw materials came from in the first place!

Many British people made good profits because of their trade connections with the British Empire.

**Raw Materials**

**Things which grew naturally or could be mined from under the ground.**

**Products**

**Those things which were made in factories.**

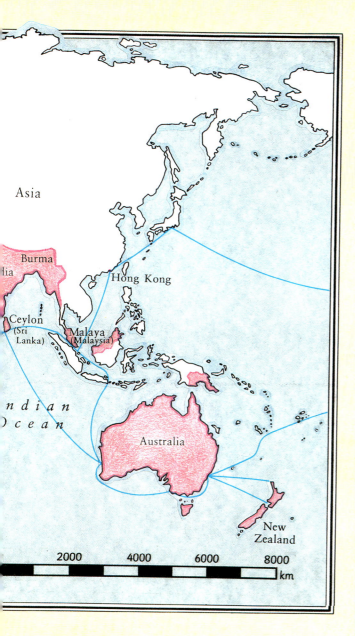

As trade increased some people left Britain to work in different parts of the Empire. This poster advertised tea and showed workers on a tea **plantation** in Sri Lanka. In Victorian times Sri Lanka was called Ceylon by the British people.

**Find:**

- the tea bushes, where workers are picking the fresh leaves.

- the warehouse on the plantation where boxes of tea are stored.

- elephants and people carrying the packed tea away from the plantation.

- a British tea planter, organising the work.

- a railway engine which took the tea to the docks.

- a box of tea being loaded on to a ship.

- the price of the tea in London.

- the badge which tells us that Queen Victoria drank the tea.

**Find:**

- the routes taken by the trade ships. The British controlled many of the ports on the main sea routes, too.

## Plantation

A large area of land planted with one crop. The word is usually used about foreign places, not Britain.

## Explorers and Missionaries

Another group of people who travelled the Empire were explorers and collectors. They wanted to be the first Europeans to travel into the interior of countries like Africa and Australia. They took measuring instruments and notebooks with them, and made maps and drawings of the places they had visited.

Africa in the nineteenth century was often called 'the white man's grave' because many Europeans died from the heat or diseases like malaria.

David Livingstone was one of the explorers who travelled many times in Africa. He was shown this big waterfall by the people who lived there. They called it Mosi-oa-tunya, but he renamed it the Victoria Falls. He also called the biggest lake in Africa, 'Lake Victoria'.

**Find:**

- the white men.

- the black Africans who showed them the way.

- the surveyor and the mapmakers, measuring and drawing.

- the 'bearers' who carried the tent and other luggage.

**Missionary**

Someone sent to do a particular job or mission.

Some explorers went to find out about the plants, animals and insects which lived in climates different from the one in Britain.

**Mary Kingsley made two journeys to Africa. She collected fishes and plants and became famous because of her book, *Travels in West Africa*.**

David Livingstone was also a missionary who wanted to **convert** the Africans to Christianity.

This picture was drawn to show people back in Britain an African king in his throne room, reading the Christian Bible.

**Find:**

- **the king reading the Bible.**

- **leopard skins. These show he is the most important man there.**

- **two British missionaries.**

- **other Africans listening to the Bible reading.**

**What is different about the clothes worn by the white men and the clothes worn by the black men?**

The Africans had gods of their own. Was it a good idea or a bad idea to try and convert them to Christianity?

---

**Convert**

**To win someone over to a cause or point of view by talking to them.**

# The Great Exhibition

In 1851, a Great Exhibition was held in London.
A special building, made of glass and iron and looking something
like a huge greenhouse, was put up in Hyde Park in London.
It was called the Crystal Palace. You can see it in this
drawing, made at the time.

**Find:**

- the Crystal Palace. What building materials were used?

- horses and riders.

- women holding sunshades. What time of year was it?

- Hyde Park.

The Exhibition was opened by Queen Victoria. Half a million people gathered in Hyde Park or inside the Palace on the opening day.

**Find:**

* the iron frame which held the building together.

* the thousands of panes of glass.

* Queen Victoria coming to open the exhibition.

On display inside were objects from all over the world. A big machine gallery was one attraction as most of the visitors had never seen a machine.

**One of the exhibits from India was a stuffed elephant and a howdah. There was also a model of the largest diamond in the world, the Koh-i-noor, which an Indian prince had given as a present to the Queen.**

**Howdah**

**A Hindi word for seat.**

# Transport and Communications

## Railways

Building the railways was one of the greatest achievements of the Victorians. An engineer called George Stephenson built the first steam **locomotive** which carried coal from the mines to the towns. In 1830, the first passenger line between Liverpool and Manchester was opened.

This painting shows the crowd at a London station in 1862.

**Find:**

- the engine, usually called the 'locomotive'.

- the container of steam to power the engine.

- the people who are going on the train and their friends and relatives saying goodbye. How would you describe their travelling clothes?

---

**Locomotive**

An engine which pulls a train. In Victorian times this was a steam engine.

---

This is the Manchester to Liverpool railway, which travelled at 30 (50 kilometres) an hour. The carriage at the end of the first-class train is an old coach which had been drawn by horses. Some people gave railway engines the nickname 'iron horses'.

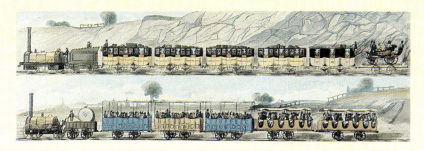

Find:

- the engines drawing the trains.

- the first class carriage for passengers who have bought the most expensive tickets.

- the second and third class travellers. What is different about the carriages built for the three different groups?

In this painting, the artist has tried to tell a story about changes in public transport in Victorian times.

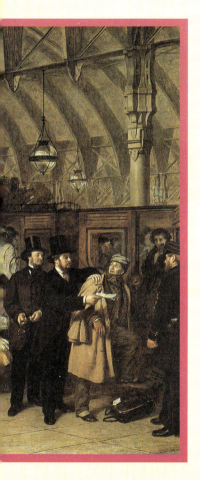

The broken-down coach was once a stage coach, which took passengers from one town to another. You can read the names of some of the towns on the side of the coach.

Can you re-tell the story:

- from the point of view of the owner of a stage coach ?

- from the point of view of the owner of a railway line ?

## Building the Railways

Engineers had the job of planning the route for a railway line. If there were mountains, hills or rivers in the way, they had to design tunnels, bridges and **viaducts**. Many people did not want the railways at first. They thought they spoilt the look of the countryside – but they soon saw how convenient they were.

**What do you think was the point of view of the artist who painted this picture of two railway lines at Armley, Leeds?**

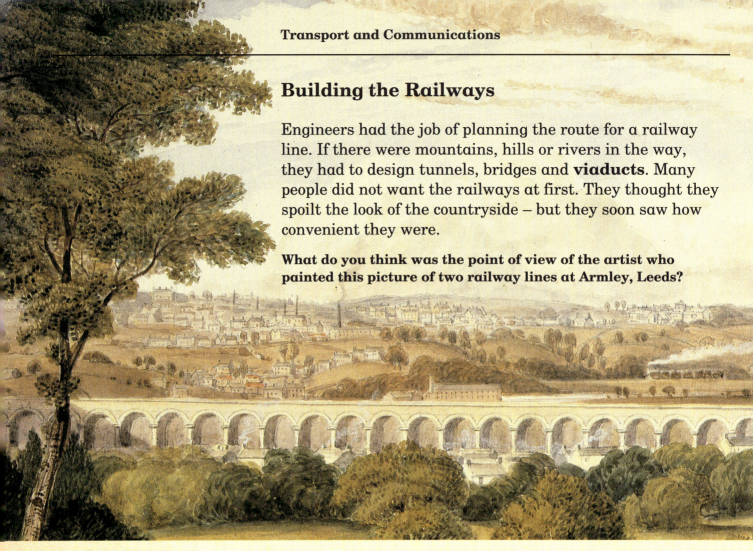

Railway navvies built the railway lines using picks, shovels and wheelbarrows. This drawing shows them at work on a cutting on the London to Birmingham line.

Find:

- navvies digging.
- planks of wood up the side of the bank.
- pulleys and horses at the top of the bank.

### Navvies

Short for 'navigators'. The name for workers who built canals and railways.

### Viaduct

A long bridge to carry a railway line above the town or countryside.

Many famous landmarks were built in the 'railway age'.

**The Forth Bridge was opened by the Prince of Wales in 1890. It took more than seven years to build and cut the journey from Edinburgh to the north of Scotland by 20 miles (about 30 kilometres).**

The railways brought many changes:

- Ordinary people could visit places they had not seen before.

- Journeys were faster and cheaper.

- More goods and people could be carried than by road transport.

- Farmers could send fresh food from the country to markets in the town.

## Steam Ships

The Victorians also found out how to build sailing ships which used steam engines. On 19 July 1843, Prince Albert went to Bristol on the train to launch the largest steam ship in the world, the SS *Great Britain*, designed by a famous engineer called Isambard Kingdom Brunel.

After the *Great Britain*, many more steam ships were built. Shipyards on the Clyde, in Belfast and in Northumberland expanded. Buildings for passengers were built at all the big ports, particularly Liverpool.

**Find:**

- **the sails. They were flown on wire cord instead of rope.**

- **the steam funnel. There were four large steam cylinders in the engine room and 24 furnaces.**

- **the ship's hull. This was made from iron plates.**

- **the sailors on board ship, waving their hats.**

- **the people of Bristol. What message about the feelings of the spectators does the picture send?**

> **Hull**
>
> **The bodywork of a steamship.**

The SS *Great Britain* was designed for the 'passenger trade'. In Victorian times this made more money for the ship owners than the transport of raw materials. Rich passengers travelled in luxury in first class. They had cabins to sleep in and spent the day in finely-decorated rooms called saloons.

Many families who had decided to **emigrate**, travelled in 'steerage class'. They spent the voyage in the lowest part of the ship, sleeping on wooden bunks. On some routes they had to take their own food. The steerage passengers were crowded together and many arrived at their destination sick and exhausted.

This picture shows passengers waving goodbye to the people they have left behind.

This painting shows what it was like to be emigrants on a ship in Victorian times.

**Emigrate**

To make a home in another country.

# Buses and trams

For most of Queen Victoria's reign, horse transport was the only way to travel in towns and cities. This drawing shows London Bridge in 1872.

**Find:**

- a two-seater carriage.

- horse-drawn waggons loaded with heavy goods. What are they carrying?

- two horse-drawn buses. How many horses were needed? Where did the passengers sit?

Around 1880 the first electric trams were introduced in many towns. These travelled on rails and got their power from overhead electric wires.

**This photograph shows a tram in Dunfermline, in Scotland.**

Electricity was also used for underground railways which were built at the end of the nineteenth century in London, Glasgow and Newcastle.

# The Post Office

Two more things helped people communicate with each other even if they did not live in the same place.

Postage stamps were first introduced in 1840. Letters and parcels could be sent on the railway and be delivered the next day. Many more people began to use the post. New Post Offices were built in all the big towns and postboxes were put up in the streets.

These people are hoping to catch the last post.

**Find:**

- **customers going to post their letters.**

- **a postman in the red uniform of the Royal Mail.**

- **a policeman controlling the crowds.**

- **sacks of mail at the back of the picture.**

- **folded newspapers being put in the post.**

Written messages could also be sent by telegrams from the Post Office. Telegrams were sent out using the telephone wires. For **sixpence**, a twelve-word message could be sent from one town to another.

The telephone was invented by Alexander Graham Bell, who was born in Edinburgh but later moved to Canada. Queen Victoria was one of the first people to have her own line.

**Sixpence**

**Two and a half p in today's money.**

# Life in the Country

## Food and Farming

The painting on this page shows a family who lived in the country. It is August and harvest time.

The artist has made it look as if they are having a holiday rather than a day of hard work.
How true a picture of the country do you think it is?

**Find:**

- the baby playing with a dog.

- the man waving to his friends.

- the bundles of corn which have been cut.

- the corn waiting to be cut.

- sickles used for cutting corn. There is one on the ground and one in the hand of a farmworker.

- the food and drink.

> **Sickle**
>
> A tool for cutting corn.

In Victorian times, everyone living in a village in the country worked in farming. They produced food, not just for themselves, but for the people who lived in the towns. Harvest time was the end of the farming year.

The harvest feast called 'Harvest Home' was paid for by the farmers. It was a way of saying 'thank-you' to all the workers and was held in the biggest barn on the farm.

ENGLISH HARVEST-HOME.

**Find:**

- **the long tables.**

- **candles to give light. The feast was held in the evening when all the work was finished.**

- **men, women and children. Everyone was invited.**

- **the barrel of beer or cider. This was made on the farm.**

The size of the harvest and the price of corn were the two things which gave the workers either a good living or a poor living for the year ahead.

## Wages

Other historical clues show that life in the countryside was not as pleasant as it looks in the pictures you have just seen.

The wages of farmworkers were much lower than money earned in a factory or on the railway. Jobs were hard and people often worked outdoors, whatever the weather. When there were bad harvests and the farmers could not sell the corn at a good price, many families nearly starved.

**Charles Sweeting from Essex was born in 1826 and spent all his life working as a farm labourer.**

**Life was hard for this Scottish woman carrying peat for her fire.
Find her cottage at the back of the photograph. It was built from peat bricks, which the family dug out for themselves.**

---

**Peat**

**Partly rotted-down plant material which can be cut into blocks, dried out and burnt as a fuel.**

| Famine |
| --- |
| **A serious shortage of food, often because a crop has failed in a whole country.** |

The 1840s were particularly hard times. They are usually called the 'Hungry Forties', particularly in Ireland where there was a terrible potato **famine**.

**Many Irish families found themselves without food or a home as a result of the potato famine.**

The wages of all members of the family were needed. Even the children were paid to do jobs on the farm like picking up stones from the fields or scaring away the birds.

These tables show the wages of one family and what they spent in 1843. The information was used by the government who wanted to find out more about life in the country in the 'Hungry Forties'.

### What they spent it on

|  |  |
| --- | --- |
| Bread | 9s. 0d |
| Potatoes | 1s. 0d |
| Rent | 1s. 2d |
| Tea | 0s. 2d |
| Sugar | 0s. 3½d |
| Soap | 0s. 3d |
| Blue for the washing | 0s. ½d |
| Thread to mend clothes | 0s. 2d |
| Candles | 0s. 3d |
| Salt | 0s. ½d |
| Coal and wood | 0s. 9d |
| Butter | 0s. ½d |
| Cheese | 0s. 3d |

### The family's wages

| Name | Age | Wage |
| --- | --- | --- |
| Robert Crick | 42 | 9s. 0d |
| His wife | 40 | 0s. 9d |
| Boy | 12 | 2s. 0d |
| Boy | 11 | 1s. 0d |
| Boy | 8 | 1s. 0d |
| Girl | 6 | |
| Boy | 4 | |

- How many people were in the family?
- How many of them had a job?
- Whose wage was the lowest?
- What did they have to eat?
- Which food item cost the most?
- What did they spend most money on after they had bought their food?

35

## Leaving the Countryside

In the nineteenth century the population of Britain increased. **Census returns** show that there were 24 million people in 1831 and 37 million in 1891.

More food was needed to feed all these people. One solution was to **import** meat from New Zealand and corn from America and Canada. Farmers and landowners also began to think of ways of producing more food more quickly in Britain.

M'CORMICK'S PATENT REAPING MACHINE,
WITH BURGESS AND KEY'S PATENT DELIVERY.

This new machine harvested the corn.

How many farmworkers were needed ?

What do you think happened to everyone else?

> ### Census returns
> Every ten years a census is taken. Everyone living in Britain has to be counted. The 'returns' are the results of the counting.

> ### Imports
> Goods bought from other countries.

Many unemployed families had to decide what to do. They could move to the town to work in a factory or emigrate to another country to start a new life. This painting shows two families thinking about emigration. Do you think the adults and the children had the same or different points of view?

Find:

- the boy in the middle of the picture. He is reading something about Australia.

- the family's possessions? How many could they take with them?

- their pet dog. What will happen to him?

- the expressions on their faces. What are they all thinking about?

Advertisements like this one went up in many country post offices. 'Agricultural workers' is another name for farmworkers.

List the things which may have persuaded the families in the painting to go to Australia.

## ADVANTAGES
### OF
## EMIGRATION
### TO
## NEW SOUTH WALES,
### OR
## EASTERN AUSTRALIA.

Farmers and small Capitalists can purchase the best FREEHOLD LAND at Six Shillings per Acre :—no Tithes, Taxes, or Rates.

The Climate is the finest in the World; there are two Crops in the Year, and the Roads and Markets are excellent.

The Passage out is safe and pleasant. Ships of large size, of the first Class, well provisioned, and carrying an able Surgeon, sail regularly every three weeks from LONDON and PLYMOUTH, for PORT-PHILIP and SYDNEY.

FOR RATES OF PASSAGE AND EVERY PARTICULAR,

## Apply to Mr. John Toms,
POSTMASTER, CHARD;

Agent to Mr. J. MARSHALL, of 26, Birchin Lane, Cornhill, LONDON.
N. B. ALL LETTERS MUST BE POST PAID.

NOTICE.----A Free Passage for Married Agricultural Labourers and Mechanics and Single Women.

TOMS, PRINTER, GAZETTE OFFICE, CHARD.

# Family Life

## Rich and Poor

The Victorians thought a lot about the family and family life.

Like Queen Victoria, most of them had more children than we have today. This painting is called Baby's Birthday and shows a family at home.

- Whose birthday is it?

- How many children are there in the family?

- What are they having for tea?

- Where is the party taking place?

- Do you think the family are rich, poor or in between?

- What else can we find out about the family and their home from the painting ?

The artist painted this family in the country.

- How large is the family?

- Are they richer or poorer than the first family? How do you know?

- Can we find anything else about their life from this painting?

This painting shows a working-class family. They are dressed plainly and do not look as if they have as much money as the two other families. The artist still managed to pose the family for the painting. How did he show that the Victorians thought families were important?

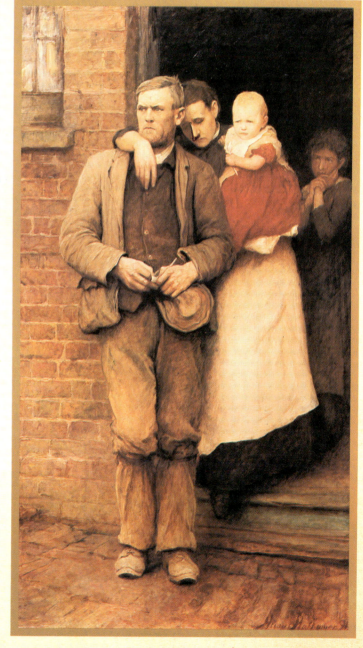

## Homes

Most Victorian families lived in small terraced houses with two rooms and a **scullery** downstairs and two bedrooms upstairs.

The toilet was outside in the back yard. People still live in the houses today, but they have had them **modernised**. Today, if we want to find out what the houses were like in Victorian times, we can visit one which has been turned into a museum.

> ### Modernised
> Made up-to-date with a bathroom and central heating.

The kitchen of a small Victorian house, built around 1890.

The family cooked and ate in this room. They only went into the front room, which they called the parlour, on Sundays.

This is the scullery or wash house.

Find:

- the sink with a cold tap.

- a plate rack.

- a 'copper'. Every Monday a fire was lit under the copper to heat water to do the washing.

- a big mangle. The washing was put through the mangle to take away some of the water.

> ### Scullery
> Sometimes called 'the back kitchen', where the sink was.

Families with more money to spend had homes with three storeys and servants to do their housework. The servants spent most of their time 'downstairs' in the kitchen in the basement while the family lived 'upstairs' in the room they called the drawing room. This room has been reconstructed in a museum to show a drawing room in the year of the Great Exhibition.

Find:

- an embroidery picture of the Crystal Palace. The women in the family did a lot of sewing like this.

- ornaments and photographs. They show the family were quite well-off.

In big houses the latest Victorian inventions such as this flush toilet were installed.

Most homes were lit with candles, but some houses had a gaslight downstairs.

These electric light bulbs came from a house called Cragside in Northumberland. It was owned by a very rich engineer called Sir William Armstrong and was the first home in Britain to have electricity.

## Children

You have read about some of the children in Britain who had to work in mines, factories or farms. The Victorians did not really agree with children working for wages. They wanted them to go to school. In 1870 a law was passed which said that schools had to be provided for all children.

Some of the first classrooms were called 'galleries'. The room was built as rows of steps so that the teacher could see all the children at once.

Some rich children had a teacher at home, called a 'governess'. Boys from wealthy families were sent to boarding schools like this one at Harrow.

## GEORGE RICHARDSON & CO.

### Central Chambers, South Castle Street, Liverpool,

Manufacturers of, and Wholesale and Retail Dealers in, MODEL STEAM ENGINES, MAGIC LANTERNS and SLIDES, METALLIC SCREW and PADDLE STEAMERS and SAILING YACHTS, TELESCOPES, MICROSCOPES, OPERA GLASSES, STEREOSCOPES and SLIDES, GLOBES, MATHEMATICAL INSTRUMENTS, BAROMETERS, THERMOMETERS, SPECTACLES, EYE and READING GLASSES, FIELD and MARINE GLASSES, MODEL TELEGRAPHS, ELECTRIC LIGHTS, TOOL CHESTS, CROQUET, all the NEW IN and OUT-DOOR GAMES, WATER COLOUR PAINTS, &c., &c., &c.

*For full Particulars of above, and Hundreds of other Articles, see Illustrated Catalogue, 112 Pages, sent free on receipt of 2 stamps.*

**METALLIC SCREW & PADDLE STEAMERS.**
Complete with Engines, &c., £6 10s. to £20 each.
*See Catalogue for full Description and Engravings as above.*

**METALLIC SAILING YACHTS.**
With Sails, Rigging, &c., complete, 6s. 6d., 13s., 16s. 6d., and 21s. each.
*See Catalogue for full Description and Engravings of above.*

**WORKING MODEL STEAM ENGINES.**
VERTICAL ENGINES, from 6s. 6d. to 31s. 6d. each.
HORIZONTAL ENGINES, from 21s. to 70s. each.
LOCOMOTIVE ENGINES, 25s., 50s., 75s., 84s., & 130s. ea.
MARINE ENGINES, both PADDLE and SCREW (for boat),
BEAM ENGINES, 100s. each.         [70s. and 105s. each.
PUMP ENGINES, 87s. 6d. each.
*See Catalogue for full Description and Engravings as above.*

**MAGIC LANTERNS AND SETS OF SLIDES.**
Complete, from 7s. 6d. to £22 each.
*See Catalogue for full Description and Engravings as above.*

**TELESCOPES.**
THE LORD BROUGHAM TELESCOPE.—Lord Brougham thinks so highly of this Telescope that he has given G. R. & Co. permission to call it as above. It will distinguish the time by a church clock five miles, and a flag-staff ten miles, landscapes thirty miles off; and will define the satellites of Jupiter and phases of Venus, &c. This extraordinary cheap and powerful glass is of the best make, and possesses Achromatic Lenses, and is equal to a Telescope that costs £5. Price 7s. 6d. each; or, carriage free, 8s. 6d.   For about 25 other varieties, ranging in price up to 84s.,
*See Catalogue, which contains full Description of the above.*

**MICROSCOPES.**
THE NEW MICROSCOPE.—This highly-finished Instrument is warranted to show the Animalculæ in water, Eels in paste, &c., magnifying some hundreds of times; it is mounted on a Brass Stand, and has a compound body, with Achromatic Lenses, Test Objects, Forceps, and Spare Glasses for mounting objects, &c. In a polished Mahogany Case complete, 7s. 6d. each; carriage free, 8s. 6d.  For about 20 other varieties, ranging in price to 63s.
*See Catalogue, which contains full Description of the above.*

### The Illustrated Catalogue.
G. R. & Co. have published a Catalogue of 112 pages, Illustrated with fourteen full-page Engravings of Steam Engines, eight Lithographed Drawings, beautifully printed in Colours, of Screw and Paddle Steamers and Sailing Yachts, and about Twenty Views of Magic Lanterns and Slides, describing upwards of 1500 varieties of Slides, embracing every subject; also full particulars of all the above-named, and many other articles; with numerous Testimonials.  Sent free on receipt of Two Stamps for postage.
Remittances must in *all cases* accompany orders.  P.O.O. payable to GEO. RICHARDSON & Co., Liverpool.

Most children had few toys apart from a bat, a ball, an iron hoop or a rope to skip with. Better-off parents could afford to buy toys for their children.

This page from a toy catalogue shows some of the new toys that were on sale.

**Find:**

- **a steam ship like the SS *Great Britain*.**

- **a model steam engine like those which pulled railway trains.**

- **a magic lantern, which showed coloured slides. The first magic lanterns worked by candlelight.**

ABC books were very popular with Victorian parents who wanted their children to learn to read.

This is one page from an ABC book. When do you think the book was written?

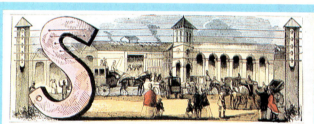

Stands for STATION, with bustle and din,
Where some folks get out, and others get in.

For the TUNNEL, that's under the ground,
Here the whistle is heard with a very long sound.

Stands for URCHIN, so simple and small,
Who cannot make out how the train goes at all.
V is for VIADUCT crossing the road,
Where the river beneath it is oft overflowed.

## Books

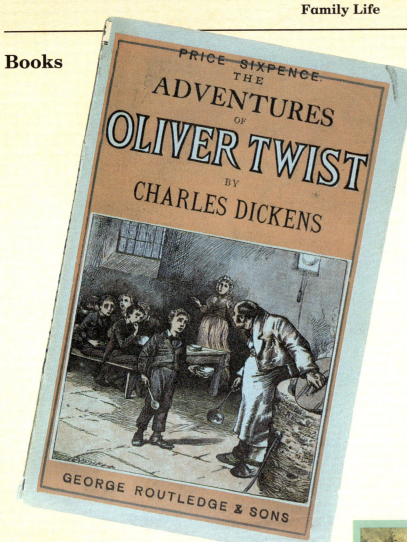

PRICE SIXPENCE.
THE
ADVENTURES
OF
OLIVER TWIST
BY
CHARLES DICKENS

GEORGE ROUTLEDGE & SONS

The first public libraries were opened in Victorian times.

The most popular stories for adults and children were written by Charles Dickens.

**Find Oliver Twist in the workhouse on the cover of the book. It was the only place to go for food if you were unemployed or had no parents.**

Two other popular children's books which adults liked reading too were *Alice in Wonderland* and *Alice Through the Looking Glass*. Alice was a real little girl, who lived in Oxford, but her adventures in the books were made up by the author who called himself Lewis Carroll.

**This picture from the book shows Alice meeting the Cheshire cat.**

# Religion

Some Victorian families were very religious. About half the population went to church or chapel on Sundays, wearing their 'Sunday best' clothes.

This photograph shows a Sunday School procession in Wales in 1880. 4,500 people took part.

Find:

- the Sunday school teachers.

- the Sunday school children.

- the terraced houses where they live.

What do you think the people who did not go to chapel thought when they saw this procession?

Some families had family prayers each morning. Every morning the family and their servants met to read the Bible and say their prayers.

The father is reading from the Bible. Both the family and the servants attended the prayers.

# Music

As there was no television or radio, people entertained each other at home. Some played the piano, others sang or, if they were very up-to-date, listened to the gramophone.

**This house belonged to a music teacher in Victorian times. Now it is part of a museum with modern people dressed in costume, pretending to be Victorian. Can you see the old gramophone in the corner?**

People who lived in a city could go out to a Music Hall or theatre. They saw a lot of different acts like short plays, acrobats, singers and magicians.

Several Comic Operas were written by Gilbert and Sullivan for performance in the theatre but people liked to sing the songs themselves at home, too.

**This is the cover of a song, which was popular over a hundred years ago.**

- **What is the song called?**
- **Where was it performed?**
- **Why do you think it was popular?**

## Sport

The Victorians were also the first to play team sports where everyone in the country followed the same rules.

The Football Association drew up its rules in 1863 and the first FA Cup Final was played in 1871.

Rules were soon fixed for the game of cricket, too, and in 1878 the first Australian touring team came to play in Britain. This photograph was taken of the team in 1878.

## Holidays

In 1871, the government decided that the first Monday in August should be made an extra public holiday for everyone. The railways made it easy for people to travel to the seaside, and the Railway Companies offered special cheap fares.

This painting shows people enjoying themselves at Ramsgate in Kent.

**Find:**

- musicians playing on the beach.

- people reading newspapers.

- a little girl having a paddle.

- some donkeys waiting for children to have a ride.

- picnic baskets.

- a pet monkey dancing on a barrel organ. This was a musical box on wheels. When the handle was turned the music played.

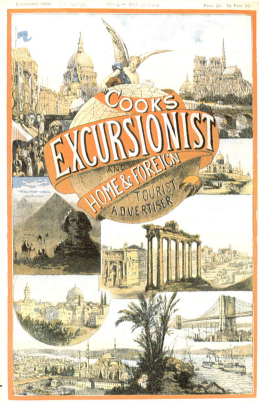

Rich people could go on some of the first package holidays arranged by Mr Thomas Cook of Leicester.